★ ★

ALASKA

by William David Thomas

GARETH**STEVENS**

GS

PUBLISHING

A Member of the WRC Media Family of Companies

D0189111

Please visit our web site at: **www.garethstevens.com**
For a free color catalog describing Gareth Stevens Publishing's
list of high-quality books and multimedia programs, call
1-800-542-2595 (USA) or 1-800-387-3178 (Canada).
Gareth Stevens Publishing's fax: (414) 332-3567.

Library of Congress Cataloging-in-Publication Data

Thomas, William, 1947-
    Alaska / William David Thomas.
       p. cm. — (Portraits of the states)
    Includes bibliographical references and index.
    ISBN-10: 0-8368-4697-4 — ISBN-13: 978-0-8368-4697-3 (lib. bdg.)
    ISBN-10: 0-8368-4714-8 — ISBN-13: 978 0-8368-4714-7 (softcover)
    1. Alaska—Juvenile literature. I. Title. II. Series.
  F904.3.T44   2006
  979.8—dc22   2006001899

This edition first published in 2007 by
Gareth Stevens Publishing
A Member of the WRC Media Family of Companies
330 West Olive Street, Suite 100
Milwaukee, WI 53212 USA

This edition copyright © 2007 by Gareth Stevens, Inc.

Editorial direction: Mark J. Sachner
Project manager: Jonatha A. Brown
Editor: Catherine Gardner
Art direction and design: Tammy West
Picture research: Diane Laska-Swanke
Indexer: Walter Kronenberg
Production: Jessica Morris and Robert Kraus

Picture credits: Cover, © Danny Lehman/CORBIS; p. 4 © Tom Bean; p. 5
© Art Today; p. 6 © Hulton Archive/Getty Images; p. 7 © Three Lions/Getty
Images; p. 9 © Bettmann/CORBIS; p. 10 © U.S. Navy/Getty Images; p. 12
© Chris Wilkins/AFP/Getty Images; pp. 15, 16 © Jeff Greenberg/PhotoEdit;
p. 18 © Pat & Chuck Blackley; pp. 21, 25, 28, 29 © AP Images; p. 22
© Susan Van Etten/PhotoEdit; p. 24 © Dave G. Houser/Post-Houserstock/
CORBIS; p. 26 © Gibson Stock Photography; p. 27 © Michael DeYoung/CORBIS

Printed in the United States of America

1 2 3 4 5 6 7 8 9 10 09 08 07 06

C O N T E N T S

Words that are defined in the Glossary appear
in **bold** the first time they are used in the text.

On the Cover: A moving wall of ice meets the ocean in Glacier Bay.
The ice in glaciers is often bright blue.

Introduction

Words like *biggest, tallest,* and *most* are often used to tell about Alaska. It is the largest of the fifty U.S. states. It has higher mountains and more oil than any other state. The list of big things about Alaska goes on and on.

The state has lots of land, but it has few people. Alaska has valleys covered with thick, moving ice. In summer, it has fields covered with flowers. Alaska has modern cities, and it has forests where bears and wolves live. It has few roads but more private airplane pilots than any other state.

Alaskans love their wild, beautiful state. Come for a visit! See what they like about being the biggest, the tallest, and the most.

Alaska's Mount McKinley is the tallest mountain in North America. Its Native Alaskan name is *Denali*. That means "high one."

The state flag of Alaska.

ALASKA FACTS

- Became the 49th U.S. State: January 3, 1959
- Population (2004): 655,435
- Capital: Juneau
- Biggest Cities: Anchorage, Juneau, Fairbanks, Sitka
- Size: 571,951 square miles (1,481,346 square kilometers)
- Nickname: The Last Frontier
- State Motto: North to the Future
- State Flower: Forget-me-not
- State Tree: Sitka spruce
- State Land Animal: Moose
- State Bird: Willow ptarmigan

5

History

Thirty thousand years ago, some hunters left their homes in Asia. They traveled across a narrow strip of land to reach Alaska. That strip, called a land bridge, is now under water.

The First Alaskans

Among the early settlers in Alaska were the Tlingit people. They lived along the southeast coast. Other people came to Alaska, too. The Haida, from Canada, were known for their beautiful carvings. The Athabascans were some of the first people to use snowshoes.

The Aleut people lived in southwestern Alaska. They built small boats, much like modern **kayaks**. An Aleut word gave the state its name. *Alyeska* means "the Great Land."

Another group of people hunted and fished in the far north. Some people called them Eskimo. They called themselves Inuit.

More than one hundred years ago, these Haida people wore special costumes for a ceremony. They are holding masks and figures carved from wood.

6

The Russian Fur Trade

In 1741, a Russian sea captain came to Alaska. His name was Vitus Bering. He saw seals and otters with thick fur. Furs were worth a lot of money then. Soon, Russian traders set up camps in Alaska.

The Russians treated the Native Alaskans badly. They killed some of the Native Alaskans. They forced others to find furs for them. Many of the Native Alaskans became sick and died from diseases that the Russians had.

The Russians stayed for more than one hundred years. Traders from other countries came to Alaska, too. Many animals were killed for their fur. Finally, the seals and otters were almost gone.

This is the Russian trading post at Sitka in 1827. From here, ships carried furs to Russia, where the furs were sold for high prices.

FACTS

Name That Town!

In 1880, a miner in southeast Alaska found lots of gold. Other miners rushed to the spot. His small camp soon became a town. The miner wanted the town to have his name. He gave lots of money to the town's people. They voted to change its name. The miner was Joe Juneau. His old camp is Alaska's capital city, Juneau.

An American Icebox

The United States was interested in Alaska's fish and **minerals**. In 1867, the United States bought Alaska from Russia. It cost just over $7 million. Many Americans thought this was foolish. They called Alaska an "icebox." Others were excited about the new land. They moved to Alaska and went to work. Fishing was the first big business. A fish **cannery** opened in 1878.

Gold!

Miners discovered gold in Alaska in the 1860s. Over the next forty years, more gold was found in this area. Miners also found gold just across the border in Canada. Thousands of people rushed north, hoping to get rich. In Alaska, stores opened to sell

IN ALASKA'S HISTORY

The Soapy Smith Gang

Soapy Smith was a famous Alaskan crook. He came to Skagway during the Gold Rush. He and his gang tricked and cheated miners to get their money. Soon, miners began staying away from Skagway. At last, the town's people had enough. They chased Smith's gang out of town. Soapy was killed in a shoot-out.

goods to the miners. Many hotels and restaurants were built. The **population** grew.

Beginnings of Government

As more people rushed to find gold, Alaskans began to think about their future. They knew they needed more laws and courts. The first code of law was written in 1900. Juneau was named the capital city the same year. The U.S. Congress made Alaska a **territory** in 1912. Soon, people wanted Alaska to be a state.

World War II

In December 1941, the United States went to war with Japan. Japanese soldiers came to Alaska. They landed on

Benny's Banner

Alaska's state flag is blue, with eight gold stars. Seven stars form the Big Dipper. The last star is the North Star. The flag was designed by John "Benny" Benson. He was a thirteen-year-old Aleut Indian boy.

Miners shovel gravel into big pans in the late 1800s. Next, the gravel is washed with water. That separates bits of gold from the sand and stones.

two islands. It was the only time during World War II that foreign soldiers took U.S. land. U.S. soldiers took the islands back from the Japanese in 1943.

Statehood

After the war, the territory of Alaska became very important. Russia and the United States had become enemies. Alaska was very close to Russia. Then, in 1957, oil was found in Alaska. More and more people wanted Alaska to be a state. Alaska became the forty-ninth U.S. state on January 3, 1959.

Oil

Prudhoe Bay is in the far northern part of Alaska. In 1968, workers there drilled holes deep

IN ALASKA'S HISTORY

The Al-Can Highway

When World War II began, there were no good roads going from the United States to Alaska . The U.S. Army began to build one. They worked twenty-four hours a day in snow, wind, and terrible cold. In just eight months, the road was finished. The Alaskan-Canadian Highway was 1,522 miles (2,449 km) long. That was more than sixty years ago. Today, the Al-Can is still the most important road going to Alaska.

These American soldiers are on Attu Island in 1943. They fought to take back the island from the Japanese in World War II.

in the earth. They found the biggest oil field in the United States. Oil brought lots of money to Alaska. Special laws were soon passed. These laws let most Alaskans share some of the oil money.

Oil brought problems, too. In 1989, an oil ship named *Exxon Valdez* ran into some rocks along the coast. The oil from the ship spilled into the ocean. Thousands of birds, otters, and other animals died. It took more than three years to clean up the oil. It cost more than $2 billion.

Today, Alaska is in the middle of a big argument. It is about land and oil. The land is the Arctic National Wildlife Refuge (ANWR). It is home to millions of **caribou** and other animals. There may be a large amount of oil under this land.

Famous People of Alaska

Susan Butcher

Born: December 26, 1956, Boston, Massachusetts

Susan Butcher grew up loving animals and the outdoors. She moved to Alaska and began raising sled dogs. She wanted to race in the famous Iditarod Trail Sled Dog Race. This race is more than 1,000 miles (1,609 km) long. Butcher entered for the first time in 1978. In one race, a moose killed two of her dogs. Butcher won the Iditarod in 1986. She went on to win the race three more times. Today, Butcher lives in Alaska with her family. She raises sled dogs and trains them to race.

Many clean-up workers helped scrub oil off seaside rocks in 1989. Oil that spilled from the *Exxon Valdez* coated many beach areas.

Some companies want to drill for the oil. Other people want to block the drilling. They think oil wells will hurt the land and animals. The argument is still going on.

IN ALASKA'S HISTORY

Native Alaskan Rights

In 1913, men from many Native groups got together. They formed the Alaskan Native Brotherhood. A group for women, the Alaskan Native Sisterhood, was formed a few years later. They worked to get back land taken by white people. They wanted the right to vote. They also wanted their children to go to good schools. In 1971, the U.S. Congress passed a special law. It was called the Alaska Native Claims Settlement Act. This law gave land and money to Native Alaskans. The law also set up twelve Native **corporations**. They protect the land and manage the money.

Early 1700s	The Haida come to Alaska many, many years after the Tlingit arrived.
1741	Vitus Bering visits Alaska. Russian fur traders soon set up small villages.
1860s	Miners find gold in Alaska and in parts of neighboring Canada. Alaska's population begins to grow.
1867	The United States buys Alaska from Russia.
1912	Alaska becomes a U.S. territory.
1942-1943	Japanese soldiers invade Alaskan islands. They are driven off by the U.S. Army.
1957	Oil is found in Alaska
1959	Alaska becomes the forty-ninth U.S. state.
1964	The strongest earthquake in U.S. history hits Alaska.
1968	The largest oil field in the United States is discovered in Prudhoe Bay.
1971	The Alaska Native Claims Settlement Act gives land and money to Native Alaskans.
1989	An oil tanker spills about 11,000,000 gallons (41,639,530 liters) of oil into the ocean near Alaska.
2006	Talks continue about drilling for oil in the Arctic National Wildlife Refuge.

People

Native Alaskans make up a big group of people in the state. They are the largest non-white group in Alaska. Most of them are Inuit and Aleut. Alaska has a higher percentage of Native citizens than any other state.

People from Many Places

Most Alaskans were not born in the state. They moved to Alaska from other places. Most of them came from other parts of the United States. Others came from

Hispanics

This chart shows the different racial backgrounds of people in Alaska. In the 2000 U.S. Census, 4.1 percent of the people in Alaska called themselves Latino or Hispanic. Most of them or their relatives came from places where Spanish is spoken. Hispanics do not appear on this chart because they may come from any racial background.

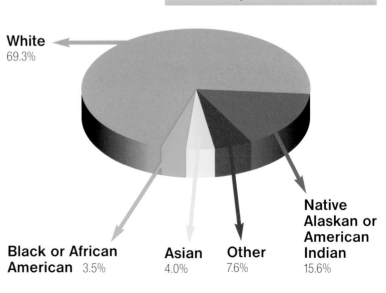

The People of Alaska

Total Population 655,435

White
69.3%

Black or African American 3.5%

Asian 4.0%

Other 7.6%

Native Alaskan or American Indian 15.6%

Percentages are based on the 2000 Census.

14

Anchorage is Alaska's biggest city. More than 260,000 people live here. It is also the main business center for the state.

Canada and Russia. Smaller numbers of people moved here from Europe and Asia.

People keep coming to Alaska. They come for lots of reasons. Many of them want to find work. The state's oil fields offer lots of jobs. Some people come for the wild, rugged land. Others move here because the state is still young and growing. Alaska is often called "the Last Frontier." People want to be part of it.

Town and Country

Alaska grew very quickly after it became a state. For many years, it grew much faster than the rest of the United States. Today, the population is still growing.

Most Alaskans now live in cities. Anchorage is the biggest city. Over 40 percent of all the people in the state

15

Alaska's capital city, Juneau, is in the southeastern part of the state. It lies between the Gulf of Alaska and two big mountains. Juneau was once a gold-mining camp. Today, more than 30,000 people live here.

live there. They work in big office buildings. They shop at malls. The children play in parks, and they go to modern schools.

Life is different in **rural** parts of the state. People often live in small villages. These areas have few roads and, sometimes, no roads at all. People travel by boats or small airplanes. During the winter, they may use dogsleds or snowmobiles.

Religion

Alaska has room for every faith. The first Alaskans had their own religions. Many Native people still follow these old faiths. When the Russians came to Alaska, they built churches. Some of these churches are still there. Today, the state has many kinds of Protestant churches. It has Roman Catholic churches, too. The state also is home to Jews, Buddhists, and people of other religions.

Education

Schools in Alaska's cities are like those in other states. In rural areas, schools may be very small, with only a few students in each grade. The state helps these students with computers. Alaskan students can connect to classes in other schools through the Internet.

The University of Alaska is the biggest university in the state. It has more than twenty-eight thousand students. The largest **campus** is in Anchorage. Other towns around the state have campuses, too. This gives many Alaskans a chance to go to college.

Famous People of Alaska

Elizabeth Peratrovich

Born: July 4, 1911, Petersburg, Alaska

Died: December 1, 1958, Juneau, Alaska

Elizabeth Peratrovich was a Tlingit Indian. When she was growing up, Native Alaskans faced **discrimination**. They could not live in some places. They could not work at some jobs. Only white people could. In 1945, Alaska's Senate was working on a new law. It would help stop discrimination. Some **senators** did not think the law was needed. Peratrovich made a speech. She told the senators how badly Native Alaskans were treated. She told them about a sign in a store. It said, "No dogs or Natives allowed." Her speech helped. The senators voted for the new law.

The Land

Alaska is separated from the rest of the United States by Canada. It is very far to the north. Fairbanks, Alaska, is almost as close to the North Pole as it is to Seattle, Washington.

Alaska is huge. It is more than twice the size of Texas, the next largest state. Alaska has long rivers, high mountains, and thick forests. It has a **panhandle** in the southeast. Alaska is a big and beautiful state.

Islands

This state has lots of islands. The Aleutian Islands reach out into the Pacific Ocean. They are farther west than any other part of the United

FUN FACTS

The Midnight Sun

In most places, daylight lasts longer on summer days than on winter days. In Alaska, summer daylight lasts almost twenty-four hours! That is why the state is called the "Land of the Midnight Sun." During the winter, however, darkness lasts nearly all day.

Mount McKinley is reflected in the waters of Wonder Lake in Denali National Park.

ALASKA

ARCTIC OCEAN

Point Barrow

Beaufort Sea

Chukchi Sea

Prudhoe Bay

Arctic National Wildlife Refugee

Brooks Range

RUSSIA

CANADA

Koyukuk R.

Yukon R.

Yukon R.

Nome

Fairbanks

Tanana R.

Denali NP

Alaska Range

Mount McKinley

Wrangell Mountains

Yukon R.

Palmer

Anchorage

Valdez

Kuskokwim R.

Iliamna L.

Haines

Skagway

Juneau

Aleutian Range

Gulf of Alaska

Sitka

Petersburg

Bering Sea

Alaska Peninsula

Ketchikan

Aleutian Islands

PACIFIC OCEAN

N

W   E

S

SCALE/KEY

0   100 Miles

0   100 Kilometers

⊛ State Capital

▲ Highest Point

▨ Mountains

States. One of the state's biggest cities is on an island. Only boats and airplanes can reach the city of Sitka.

Mountains

Alaska has many mountains. The Brooks Range crosses the state in the north. One southern range is the Alaska Range. Mount McKinley is in this range. At 20,320 feet (6,194 meters) high, it is North America's tallest peak.

The Central Region

Between Alaska's mountain ranges is the central region. This is a large, hilly area. It is full of river valleys and **muskeg**. Muskeg is a kind of swampy, soggy soil. The Yukon River runs through the central region. It is the longest river in the state.

The Coastal Plain

In the far northern part of Alaska is the Arctic coastal

Major Rivers
Yukon River
1,979 miles (3,184 km) long
Kusokwim River
600 miles (965 km) long
Tanana River
550 miles (885 km) long

plain. This region has many of Alaska's oil wells, but not many people. It is one of the coldest parts of Alaska. Much of the land is frozen all year long. Land like this is called **permafrost**. Point Barrow is in this area. It is farther north than any other part of the United States.

Earthquakes

Alaska has more earthquakes than the rest of the United States put together. In 1964, the state was rocked by a huge earthquake. It was the strongest ever to hit the United States. Anchorage and several other towns were very badly damaged.

Plants and Animals

Trees cover one-third of Alaska. The state tree is the Sitka spruce. It grows near the sea. In summer, Alaska's fields and plains are covered with wildflowers.

Alaska is a great place for animal watchers. Herds of caribou travel across the state each year. Moose, elk, beavers, wolves, and musk oxen live here. Alaska also is the home of some of the world's largest bears. It has Kodiak, grizzly, black, and polar bears.

More bald eagles live in Alaska than in all the other states. Salmon and trout swim in the rivers and lakes. Otters and seals play in the sea. Whales glide in the ocean.

FUN FACTS

Fire and Ice

When many people think of volcanoes, they think of Hawaii. In fact, Alaska has nearly 80 percent of all the active volcanoes in the United States. Alaska also has many glaciers. These are huge, slow-moving masses of ice. Two of the state's glaciers each cover more land than the whole state of Delaware!

This mother grizzly bear and her cubs are looking for fish along an Alaskan river. Grizzlies are beautiful, but they can be very dangerous.

Economy

Much of the money made in Alaska comes from the land. Oil, forests, and fish are the most important **natural resources** in the state. The people in Alaska want to protect these resources. They try to use them wisely.

Black Gold

Oil and natural gas are the most valuable resources in Alaska. They are important to the state's economy. Most of Alaska's oil comes from the far north. From there, the oil travels through a pipeline. It goes

This ship is in the port of Valdez. It's being loaded with oil from the Trans Alaska Pipeline System.

over 800 miles (1,287 km) to seaports in the south. The oil takes six days to go from one end of the pipeline to the other.

Forests, Fish, and Farms

Alaska's forests and fish are other important resources. Trees from forests are made into lumber and paper. Fish provide food. More fish are caught in Alaska than in any other state.

Alaska has some farms. In summer, the sun shines almost all day long. Often, the vegetables grow very large. Some carrots weigh 15 pounds (6.8 kilograms)!

Services

The biggest number of Alaskans have service jobs. People who teach, cook, and help tourists work in service jobs. Doctors and nurses are service workers, too.

How Money Is Made in Alaska

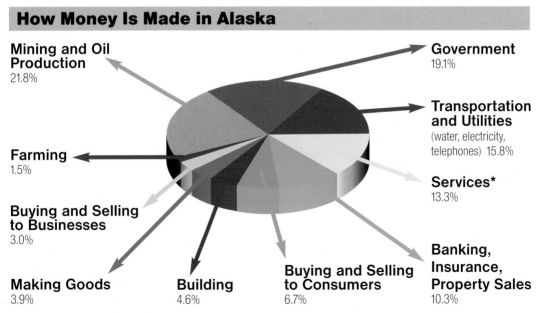

Mining and Oil Production
21.8%

Government
19.1%

Transportation and Utilities
(water, electricity, telephones) 15.8%

Farming
1.5%

Services*
13.3%

Buying and Selling to Businesses
3.0%

Banking, Insurance, Property Sales
10.3%

Making Goods
3.9%

Building
4.6%

Buying and Selling to Consumers
6.7%

* Services include jobs in hotels, restaurants, auto repair, medicine, teaching, and entertainment.

23

Government

Alaska's state government is like the government of the United States. It has three parts, or branches.

Executive Branch

The executive branch carries out the laws of the state. It is led by the governor. The lieutenant governor helps the governor. Many other officials also work in this branch.

Legislative Branch

The legislative branch of the state government makes the laws. This

A statue of a brown bear guards the State Capitol Building in Juneau.

branch has two parts. They are the Senate and the House of Representatives.

Judicial Branch

Courts and judges make up the judicial branch. They may decide whether a person who is accused of committing a crime is guilty. In Alaska, all courts are run by the state, rather than by towns or cities.

Local Governments

Alaskan cities have a mayor and a city council. Native corporations also are part of Alaska's local government. They help manage and protect the land, rights, and money of Native Alaskans.

ALASKA'S STATE GOVERNMENT

Executive		Legislative		Judicial	
Office	Length of Term	Body	Length of Term	Court	Length of Term
Governor	4 years	Senate (20 members)	4 years	Supreme (5 justices)	3, then 10 years
Lieutenant Governor	4 years	House of Representatives (40 members)	2 years	Court of Appeals (3 judges)	3, then 8 years

Things to See and Do

I n a state with the biggest, the tallest, and the most, you'll never run out of things to see and do.

Museums and Parks

You can learn about Alaska's past at one of its great museums. The State Museum in Juneau tells about the history of this big state. It also has displays about Native Alaskan **culture**. At the Fairbanks Dog Mushing Museum, you can learn about sled dog racing. You can find out about the years of the Gold Rush at a historical park in Skagway.

A Native Alaskan carves a totem pole in Saxman Village, near Ketchikan.

Many hikers and climbers visit Denali National Park. In all, Alaska has fifteen national parks. They are great places to camp, hike, and enjoy the scenery.

Let's Celebrate!

Alaskans celebrate all year long. In fall, you can visit Haines for the Bald Eagle Festival. Check out the Ice Climbing Festival in Valdez in winter. In spring, go to the Festival of Native Arts in Fairbanks. You will see art and dancing by Native Alaskans. Alaska's State Fair takes place in Palmer every summer. You can enjoy games, rides, and animals.

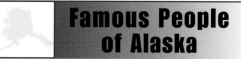

Famous People of Alaska

Jewel

Born: Born: May 23, 1974, Payson, Utah

Jewel Kilcher moved to Alaska when she was very young. By age six, she was singing on stage with her parents. She became well known in 1989. She sang "Over the Rainbow" on a popular radio show. Her first album, *Pieces of You*, was released in 1995. Since then, Jewel has sung all over the country. She also has written two books.

Hikers on snowshoes watch the Northern Lights flash above the mountains.

Sports

Alaskans play all kinds of sports. The Eskimo-Indian Olympics take place in Fairbanks each year. These are tests of Native Alaskan skills. Each summer, at the Midnight Sun Baseball Classic in Fairbanks, games are played at night, without any lights! In November, college basketball comes to Anchorage. Some of the top teams compete in the Great Alaska Shootout.

Famous People of Alaska

Jack London

Born: January 12, 1876, San Francisco, California

Died: November 22, 1916, Santa Rosa, California

Jack London came to Alaska and the Yukon in 1897. He was looking for gold, but he found ideas for stories. He wrote about many of the people and things he saw in the far north. His writing made him famous. One of London's best-known books is *The Call of the Wild*. It is about a big dog named Buck. Another book he wrote, *White Fang*, is about a wolf. Both stories have been made into movies.

Melissa Rima from the city of North Pole gets past Hillarie Putnam from Wasilla and goes for the basket. The girls are competing in a high school playoff game in Anchorage.

Jeff King guides his team in the 2006 Iditarod Trail Sled Dog Race. This famous race is more than 1,000 miles (1,609 km) long. King and his dogs have won the Iditarod three times.

Snowmobiling, skiing, snowshoeing, and other winter sports are popular. The official state sport is sled dog racing. These races take place all winter long. The Iditarod Trail Sled Dog Race is the most famous. It takes from eight to fourteen days to finish this long race.

FUN FACTS

Racing Against Time

In January 1925, people in Nome were sick and dying. The medicine they needed was in Anchorage. That was almost 700 miles (1,127 km) away. All of the roads were closed. Airplanes could not be used. In Anchorage, a man put the medicine on his dogsled. He started for Nome as fast as he could go. He passed the medicine to another dog team. In all, twenty brave men and their dogs ran for six days in cold, snow, and darkness. The medicine got to Nome in time to help the people. Today, the Iditarod Trail Sled Dog Race remembers those men.

campus — the buildings and land that belong to a school

cannery — a factory where food is put into cans

caribou — a kind of very large deer

corporations — large businesses

culture — the language, beliefs, and actions of a people

discrimination — treating people badly because of their race or religion

kayaks — small boats, usually for just one person

minerals — valuable materials found on or under the ground, such as gold or oil

muskeg — soft, wet soil found in parts of Alaska

natural resources — valuable things found in nature that can be used by people, such as trees, fish, or oil

panhandle — a narrow area of land that juts out from the rest of the state

permafrost — ground that is frozen all year long

population — the number of people who live in a place, such as a state

rural — far away from big cities and large towns

senators — people elected to make laws

territory — an area of land that belongs to a country